Yada Yada

A DEVOTIONAL JOURNAL

FOR MOMS

Yada Yada

A DEVOTIONAL JOURNAL FOR MOMS

Vicki Courtney

FOUNDER OF VIRTUOUS REALITY MINISTRIES
AND YADA YADA EVENTS

Broadman & Holman Publishers
NASHVILLE, TENNESSEE

Yada Yada: A Devotional Journal for Moms

ISBN 0-8054-3058-X

Broadman & Holman Publishers
Nashville, Tennessee
broadmanholman.com

Dewey Decimal Classification: 242.643
Mothers–Diaries / Spiritual Journals / Diaries

Printed in Korea
1 2 3 4 07 06 05 04

Contents

Introduction

I'm thrilled that you have picked up this book, because I believe there is only one thing our daughters need more than a mother who is devoted to them—and that's a mother who's even *more* devoted to God.

President John Adams once said, "From all that I had read of history and government of human life and manners, I had drawn this conclusion: that the manners of women were the most infallible barometer to ascertain the degree of morality and virtue of a nation." If this is true, we have received a high calling as mothers of daughters. One look at the magazine rack at the supermarket checkout should convince most mothers that we have a long way to go when it comes to the "manners of women."

I've had it with the culture's negative influences on our girls, and I'm willing to bet that you have, too. It's time for mothers of daughters to unite with purpose. It's time to step forward and refuse to allow the world to take our girls by the hand and lead them through life.

I know that the experiences we'll share in the days ahead will give you renewed hope and confidence in Christ. I know it will make your time with your daughter more purposeful and enriching. This calling of ours—to raise godly daughters in an ungodly world—is near and dear to the Father's heart, and I know He will give us what we need to achieve it.

So let's venture out together into His Word and His truth. Let us begin by asking God to lead the way in the pursuit to raise our daughters to be, above all, His girls. While we're at it, let's be bold enough to ask God to leave us forever changed by the time we turn the last page.

Whose Child Is This?

One of the most beautiful accounts of maternal love found in Scripture is the story of Hannah. Barren for many years, Hannah cried out to God for a son and vowed to give him over to God, if God would comply by meeting her request. God did indeed bless her with a son, Samuel. And true to her word, she cared for him until he was weaned, then brought him to Eli, the priest, to live out the remainder of his childhood years at the temple.

After he was weaned, she took the boy, young as he was . . . and brought him to the house of the LORD. . . . They brought the boy to Eli, and she said to him, "As surely as you live, my lord, I am the woman who stood here beside you praying to the LORD. I prayed for this child, and the LORD has granted me what I asked of him. So now I give him to the LORD. For his whole life he will be given over the the LORD."
1 Samuel 1:24–28

What mother could take a child she had nursed at her breast, swayed to sleep in her arms, watched as he took his first wobbly steps—and then put him in the care of a stranger, releasing him to the plans of God? Only a woman desperately dependent on Him.

WIDER ANGLE

Read 1 Samuel 1. Watch for verses:
8 (the pain of being misunderstood)
11 (the passion of a desperate prayer)
18 (the right way to leave a request with God)
28 (our proper response to every situation: worship)

My Page

Hannah's story makes me wonder how much of what I desire for my daughter is just my personal wants and wishes, and how much of it is what God desires for her . . .

Train a child in the way he should go,
and when he is old he will not turn from it.
Proverbs 22:6

Her Page

Here's what I'd like to say to my daughter about the safety of being in God's will—but also about the struggle it is for me to trust in Him myself sometimes.

The L*ORD is the stronghold of my life—*
of whom shall I be afraid.
Psalm 27:1

God's Page

Lord, it's a great privilege to have one of your children right here where I can love her, and lead her, and watch what you are doing in her. Today I pray . . .

Trust in the LORD *with all your heart and lean not on your own understanding.*

Proverbs 3:5

Fool Me Once

It's hard to be a girl in today's culture. Our sex-crazed society has been in the making for several decades. If you were to trace its roots, you would find the radical women's liberation movement coupled with the sexual revolution at the helm. Both have contributed greatly to the moral free fall in our country by promoting sexual and personal freedom at the cost of family and social virtue. The Bible talks about how to respond to mindsets like these:

Do not deceive yourselves. If any one of you thinks he is wise by the standards of this age, he should become a "fool" so that he may become wise. For the wisdom of this world is foolishness in God's sight. As it is written: "He catches the wise in their craftiness"; and again, "The Lord knows that the thoughts of the wise are futile."
1 Corinthians 3:18–20

Both we and our daughters need to know that the standards set by the world around us should never be taken at face value. In fact, we are told in Scripture to question the things society accepts, to be suspicious when what comes naturally is what also becomes the norm.

WIDER ANGLE

Read Isaiah 5:8–24. Watch for verses:
12 (the age-old root cause of selfish desires)
14 (the range of people who embrace worldliness)
17 (God's promise of protection for the righteous)
20 (the theme of this whole section)

My Page

If I could name the ways I've been negatively affected by the fallout of the radical women's movement and the sexual revolution, these are the ones I'd say are the most noticeable, the most damaging:

He feeds on ashes, a deluded heart misleads him; he cannot save himself, or say, "Is not this thing in my right hand a lie?"
Isaiah 44:20

Her Page

The underlying word here is *deception.* What are some things I can do for my daughter, some examples I could point out, that would show her how easy it is for us to be deceived by the culture?

Encourage one another daily . . .

so that none of you may be hardened by sin's deceitfulness.

Hebrews 3:13

God's Page

Lord, I need You to show me the areas in my life where I am still being deceived, places where I've bought into the world's way of thinking. My prayer about this today is . . .

Whoever follows me will never walk in darkness, but will have the light of life.

John 8:12

That Empty Feeling Inside

The radical women's liberation movement that took place in our day has evolved into the domineering and aggressive "girl power" movement of today. Peddled through teen fashion magazines, media, and the education system, the message is clear: It's all about you. You can have it all. You set the rules. Do whatever feels good and gets you what you want. The problem is, this is not what women really *want.* I talk to countless teens, college women, and others who have unknowingly bought into the "girl power" message, only to find themselves feeling empty in the end.

He saved them from the hand of him who hated them, and redeemed them from the hand of the enemy. . . . Then they believed His words. They sang His praise. But they soon forgot His works; they did not wait for His counsel, but lusted exceedingly in the wilderness, and tested God in the desert. And He gave them their request, but sent leanness into their soul.
Psalm 106:10, 12–15 (NKJV)

It happens so often. We think we know what we want, we think we know what's best for us, and God in His fatherly love allows us to choose our own path. But it never quite turns out the way it was advertised. We're left instead with a noticeable "leanness" in our souls.

WIDER ANGLE

Read Psalm 106. Watch for verses:
7 (we come from a long line of amnesia victims)
16 (envy—the sin that tends to make us deaf to God)
23 (the power of one who dares to speak truth)
44 (the mercy of God, His desire to redeem us)

My Page

I'm amazed at how short my memory of God's blessing in my life can be—and how often I am left "lean" in my soul. Just to help me be less forgetful, I need to list some of the things He's done for me:

Were I to count them, they would outnumber the grains of sand.
Psalm 139:18

Her Page

My *daughter* and I need to remember about God's blessings, too. I think I'll sit down with her real soon and see if she'll help me come up with some other ways God has protected and provided for us:

Praise the L*ORD*, *O my soul, and forget not all his benefits.*

Psalm 103:2

God's Page

Lord, I know what it's like to feel "lean" in my soul. But I must say that I'm thankful to You even for that, because You always use it to draw me back to You. I praise You, Lord, for this . . .

But seek first his kingdom and his righteousness, and all these things will be given to you as well.
Matthew 6:33

Going God's Way

I want my daughter to know that man-generated movements will come and go, but the movement God began with the death of His Son will never die out. True "liberation" can only come in knowing the One who died to set men free. For too many girls today, the search for something to fill the giant hole in their hearts is leading them from one thing to another, with emptiness and disappointment always waiting for them at the end. If the way they choose is not Christ, it's a counterfeit.

Stand at the crossroads and look; ask for the ancient paths, ask where the good way is, and walk in it, and you will find rest for your souls.
Jeremiah 6:16

Our girls are in need of new direction. They are longing for rest in their souls. They are desiring a relationship with someone who will love and protect them. We know who this "Someone" is. We know the "good way." We have seen enough of life to know that this is the only way that leads to peace, rest, hope, and contentment. For the sake of our daughters, then, we must not rest until we've made this way plain to them. We who have been given the blessing of knowing the "good way" ourselves must share the joy we have found in walking with Christ.

WIDER ANGLE

Read Jeremiah 6:16–19. Watch for verses:
16 (spoken from a reliable and trustworthy source)
16B (the formula for happiness, yet the people said . . .)
17 (the modern day equivalent of plugging our ears)
19 (stubbornness often yields consequences)

My Page

I've known several people in my life who have modeled the good way" to me. Here are their names, and here's how they did it:

It is to be a witness between us and you and the generations that follow.

Joshua 22:27

Her Page

If I had to describe to my daughter what it is to be "liberated," I'd tell her this:

If the Son sets you free, you will be free indeed.

John 8:36

God's Page

Father, I praise You for going to such extraordinary lengths to make the "good way" known to us. In the hopes that my daughter and I would walk in the "good way," I pray today . . .

My feet have closely followed his steps;
I have kept to his way without turning aside.
Job 23:11

And . . . Action!

Given the times, it is more important than ever that we parents are purposeful about the spiritual training of our children. It's not enough anymore—if it ever was—to simply take them to church, teach them the Golden Rule, and say routine bedtime prayers over them. As mothers appointed by God to raise His children in today's world, we must set forth His principles with purpose and determination. We must be serious and consistent in making sure the Word of God is a big part of their daily lives.

These commandments that I give you today are to be upon your hearts. Impress them on your children. Talk about them when you sit at home and when you walk along the road, when you lie down and when you get up. Tie them as symbols on your hands and bind them on your foreheads. Write them on the doorframes of your houses and on your gates.
Deuteronomy 6:6–9

To begin with, we must strive to have a clearer understanding of God's truths ourselves, so that we can be effective in impressing them on the hearts of our children—teaching them with our words and showing them with our actions. We must practice what we preach and preach what we practice.

WIDER ANGLE

Read Deuteronomy 6. Watch for verses:
12 (our tendency to let his teachings grow stale)
18 (the promise of blessing attached to our obedience)
20 (the dialogue God expects between parents and children)
24 (keep track of the ways obedience has paid off)

My Page

Sometimes I find myself talking to my daughter about everything else but the Word of God, not being watchful for ways to apply it to her life. What keeps me from doing that?

For a long time I have been silent;

I have been quiet and held myself back.

Isaiah 42:14

Her Page

If I just take an average week into consideration, I can think of several opportunities where my daughter and I could make better use of our time together, like:

We were delighted to share with you

not only the gospel of God but our lives as well.

1 Thessalonians 2:8

God's Page

Lord, I want so badly to be more free, less afraid, and more effective in bringing Your Word alive in my daughter's life—and in my own. I ask you today for . . .

You accepted it not as the word of men, but as it actually is, the word of God.

1 Thessalonians 2:13

Too Busy

Busyness is a way of life, but the truth is, we make time for the things we deem to be important. And I can't imagine *anything* more important than the spiritual training of our daughters. I'm not saying for a second that the benefits of team sports, music lessons, and a good education won't be helpful in our daughters' lives for years to come. But training them to walk in God's ways will have a greater impact on them than all of these other activities put together—not just for now, but for all eternity.

The end of all things is near. Therefore be clear minded and self-controlled so that you can pray. Above all, love each other deeply, because love covers over a multitude of sins. . . . If anyone speaks, he should do it as one speaking the very words of God. If anyone serves, he should do it with the strength God provides, so that in all things God may be praised.
1 Peter 4:7–8, 11

My husband and I have often had to tell our children "no" about participating in activities that in themselves were fine and good—because by saying "yes," we would have produced a pace too frenzied to leave room for their spiritual training. It's a tough call, but so is the calling God has given us.

WIDER ANGLE

Read Luke 8:40–56. Watch for verses:
42 (the way Jesus can relate to our time pressure)
46 (His ability to be all there, wherever He was)
48 (peace—it's what He offers us, if we'll take it)
50 (we may be in a big hurry, but God isn't)

My Page

I'm not exactly sure how to free up our family's schedule, but here are some ideas that come to mind, some issues we need to consider before we commit to one more thing:

Commit to the L*ORD* *whatever you do,*

and your plans will succeed.

Proverbs 16:3

Her Page

If I were to sit down with my daughter to discuss her schedule, here are some of the things I'd like to talk about, some of the bigger reasons for not being so jam-packed and busy:

You expected much, but see,

it turned out to be little.

Haggai 1:9

God's Page

Lord, I bring our family's calendar before You today and lay it at Your feet. It needs Your touch on it, Lord. It needs to be centered around You, not us. Help us, Father, to . . .

Many are the plans in a man's heart,

but it is the L*ORD's purpose that prevails.*

Proverbs 19:21

Friendly Fire

We do our daughter a great disservice when we are more concerned with being her "friend" than being her "mom." It's only natural for us to want to be loved and appreciated by others, especially by our children. And it is possible to be both mom and friend to them, but it definitely takes a fine balancc. Jesus put this matter into startling perspective when He told His followers that harmony at all costs is not the grand goal of Christian living.

Do not suppose that I have come to bring peace to the earth. I did not come to bring peace, but a sword. For I have come to turn "a man against his father, a daughter against her mother, a daughter-in-law against her mother-in-law. . . ." Anyone who loves his father or mother more than me is not worthy of me; anyone who loves his son or daughter more than me is not worthy of me.

Matthew 10:34–35, 37

What a pleasure and privilege it is to enjoy our daughters, to develop that kind of close bond between us. But we are called upon by God to draw firm lines in the sand at times, lines that can often threaten the feel-good relationship between us. We must be willing to be what they need in a mother, not what they want in a friend.

WIDER ANGLE

Read Galatians 2:11–21. Watch for verses:
11 (sometimes, it is "clearly" right to confront)
13 (there are ramifications on others if we let things go)
14 (we must challenge our daughters to live their faith)
20 (our first allegiance is always to Christ—always!)

My Page

It wasn't the "cool" thing to do, but I can remember a time when I had to put aside my desire to be liked by my daughter and her friends, and to do something unpopular:

It is time for judgment to begin with the family of God.

1 Peter 4:17

Her Page

I wondered how my daughter really felt about moms who bend over backwards to try to fit in. When I asked her about that, here's what she said:

Each of you must respect his mother and father.

Leviticus 19:3

God's Page

Lord, I pray for the courage to stand up to my children, even when it causes friction. And I pray for the wisdom to know when to back off, when I'm taking it too far. I have a lot to pray for, Lord . . .

Your servant has found courage to offer you this prayer.

2 Samuel 7:27

What You Don't Know

If we are to adequately train our daughters in the Christian faith, we must be well acquainted with the Christian's training manual for living. The Bible is the best-selling book of all time, but it too often earns a spot up on a shelf rather than in the center of a life. If we are to teach our daughters to walk in His ways, we must become students of His Word.

The unfolding of your words gives light; it gives understanding to the simple. I open my mouth and pant, longing for your commands. Turn to me and have mercy on me, as you always do to those who love your name. Direct my footsteps according to your word; let no sin rule over me. . . . Make your face shine upon your servant and teach me your decrees.
Psalm 119:130–133, 135

Once we dive into God's Word, it is easy to become overwhelmed with what we don't know. We must not allow our feelings of inadequacy, however, to prevent us from passing on what we *do* know. I am driven to become a devoted student of God's Word by the frightening realization that my ability to effectively verbalize the ways of God will impact my family for generations. If we desire to raise daughters who are desperately dependent on God's Word, we must model to them that we, too, are desperately dependent on His Word.

WIDER ANGLE

Read Psalm 119:1–24. Watch for verses:
5–6 (the secret of understanding God's Word—obeying it!)
9 (how essential the Bible is to our children's character)
11 (the discipline of committing Scripture to memory)
18 (praying for God's insight and trusting Him to give it)

My Page

How would my priorities need to change in order to make more time for Bible study? I know what a blessing it's been whenever I've committed to doing it more faithfully.

Accept instruction from his mouth,
and lay up his words in your heart.
Job 22:22

Her Page

I'm afraid that sometimes my daughter feels like she's heard all of this before, that although she loves the Lord, His Word seems sort of tired and irrelevant. What would she say to that assessment?

I have been reminded of your sincere faith,
which first lived in your grandmother . . . and in your mother.
2 Timothy 1:5

God's Page

Oh Lord, I want so badly to be a better student of Your Word, to learn my way around the Bible better and to put my faith and beliefs into words. Will You help me, Lord? I pray that You'll . . .

If any of you lacks wisdom, he should ask God who gives generously to all without finding fault.
James 1:5

What's the Big Deal?

I continue to be amazed that—even with all the disturbing trends in our society, even with all the shocking write-ups in our newspapers, even with the things kids are wearing today at the average mall food court—some Christian parents are still not able to see that we're in trouble here . . . and that our children are the ones suffering the most for it. It is not prudish and judgmental to look around at the shape of our nation today and conclude that the ways of the world are failing. Dangerously.

Mark this: There will be terrible times in the last days. People will be lovers of themselves, lovers of money, boastful, proud, abusive, disobedient to their parents, ungrateful, unholy, without love, unforgiving, slanderous, without self-control, brutal, not lovers of the good, treacherous, rash, conceited, lovers of pleasure rather than lovers of God. . . . Have nothing to do with them.

2 Timothy 3:1–5

I've heard it said that the best time to plant a tree is ten years ago; the second best time is now! Yes, as Christians, we should have acted sooner to counteract these negative influences in our culture. But while we can't go back, we can go forward—taking our children with us in pursuit of righteousness.

WIDER ANGLE

Read Romans 1:18–32. Watch for verses:
19 (mankind's awareness of God and His standards)
24 (God's response to our willful sin)
26 (the long history of deviance and perversion)
32 (our willingness to accept evil as ordinary and okay)

My Page

Of all the things that distress me the most about the world my daughter is growing up in, these are the ones that frighten me the most:

They have given themselves over to sensuality . . .

with a continual lust for more.

Ephesians 4:19

Her Page

My daughter and I have talked a lot about today's cultural trends, to help her deal with all the things she's hearing and seeing in today's world. This is what I keep telling her:

Anyone who chooses to become a friend of the world becomes an enemy of God.

James 4:4

God's Page

Lord, there's part of me that would like to stick my head in the sand and act as though things aren't as bad as they are. There's also part of me that just wants to smother my children. What do I do, Lord?

In regard to evil be infants, but in your thinking be adults.
1 Corinthians 14:20

He'll Be There

The current plight we face today in the culture department is no different than it was in Old Testament times, when God's people succumbed to the negative influences of those around them and found themselves empty and lacking direction. But God continued to receive His people back when they returned to Him. He was always there to restore and reestablish them. So we have reason for hope when we consider Who is on our side, One who has wired our hearts for fellowship with Him.

As the rain and the snow come down from heaven, and do not return to it without watering the earth and making it bud and flourish, so that it yields seed for the sower and bread for the eater, so is my word that goes out from my mouth: It will not return to me empty, but will accomplish what I desire and achieve the purpose for which I sent it.
Isaiah 55:10–11

So let us make certain that we have returned to the Lord. Let us be sure that our hearts are fully in His hand, that we are continually seeking Him along with and for our children, and that although we see much to *concern* us, we see much more to *encourage* us that God will be our strength and shield.

WIDER ANGLE

Read Isaiah 55:1–13. Watch for verses:
1 (God's desire to feed us at His own expense)
3 (the forever covenant promises of a loving God)
8 (His ability to do whatever He desires with us)
13 (what the transforming power of God looks like)

My Page

I've had to return to God many times in my life. And He has never failed to be there for me, His arms outstretched, His love unwavering. I remember one time in particular:

If my people would but listen to me . . .
how quickly would I subdue their enemies.
Psalm 81:13–14

Her Page

I hope that in those times when my daughter has had to come to me, apologetic and repentant, that I have dealt with her the way God deals with me. How can I show her this more clearly?

"Return to me, and I will return to you,"

says the LORD Almighty.

Malachi 3:7

God's Page

Father, You have always been there for me—through my growing-up years, my teenage years, now into my adult years. All I know to do is to praise You for a love so faithful and true . . .

Jesus Christ is the same yesterday and today and forever.

Hebrews 13:8

The Trail of Tears

When we as mothers humble ourselves before God and weep before Him, crying out for help and direction, He will have mercy and hear our prayers. It is good to cry. It's a sign that the passion we feel for our daughters to become godly, virtuous young women has worked its way down into the center of our hearts. Our worldly culture is exposing our girls to situations they are not equipped to handle. They are being forced to grow up too fast. We have no choice but to go to God and plead for their protection.

Jesus told his disciples a parable to show them that they should always pray and not give up. . . . And the Lord said, "Listen to what the unjust judge says. Will not God bring about justice for his chosen ones, who cry out to him day and night? Will he keep putting them off? I tell you, he will see that they get justice, and quickly. However, when the Son of Man comes, will he find faith on the earth?"

Luke 18:1, 6–8

We have God's promise that He will respond to our prayers. We, then, must make a point to ask Him in our prayer times to break our hearts, to show us all that we need to see in order to pray effectively for our children, to give us spirits so full of love that we will go to any lengths to care for them.

WIDER ANGLE

Read Luke 6:12–26. Watch for verses:
12 (the need that Jesus Himself felt for prayer)
21 (now is not the time to indulge ourselves)
23 (God's mysterious surprise of joy to the sorrowful)
25 (the end result of those who don't understand the times)

My Page

The last time I absolutely pled with God concerning my children's situation and the times in which we live, I was overwhelmed because:

This is why I weep and my eyes overflow with tears.

Lamentations 1:16

Her Page

I'm not sure if my daughter knows how often my heart breaks over the challenges she has to face in today's culture. Here's what I'd like to tell her about that:

My spirit grows faint within me;

my heart within me is dismayed.

Psalm 143:4

God's Page

Father, I will not be ashamed to come before You with a tear-streaked face, because You know my heart. You know my deepest desires. And so I come again today, asking, praying . . .

Let your ear be attentive and your eyes open to hear the prayer your servant is praying before you day and night.

Nehemiah 1:6

Clinging to Covenant

The most defining moment in King Josiah's reign came when he was in his mid-twenties. After years of spiritual decay in the generations before him, Josiah ordered that the land of Israel be purified of idolatry. And while doing some repair work in the temple, the Book of the Law was found—dusty and worn from decades of going unheeded. Broken and convicted by this providential find, the young king ordered that a special ceremony be held for all the people of the land. And here's what happened:

He read in their hearing all the words of the Book of the Covenant, which had been found in the temple of the LORD. The king stood by the pillar and renewed the covenant in the presence of the LORD—to follow the LORD and keep his commands, regulations and decrees with all his heart and soul, thus confirming the words of the covenant written in this book. Then all the people pledged themselves to the covenant.
2 Kings 23:2–3

Many of the mother/daughter battles we face are already settled in advance when we as moms choose to adhere to the standards of God's Word. While it is important that we not get carried away, legalistically following the letter of the law, it is also important that we not ignore its teachings in our homes.

WIDER ANGLE

Read 2 Kings 23:1–25. Watch for verses:
12 (the only way to dispose of temptations)
17 (undying respect for those who stand up for God)
21 (our need for celebrating and remembering)
25 (the wrap-up on Josiah's work, his heart for God)

My Page

This idea of "covenant" is fascinating to me, because its roots go back so far into our history, and yet God is still maintaining covenant with us even today. As I've read these verses about covenant, it's made me think that . . .

He is the faithful God, keeping his covenant of love to a thousand generations of those who love him and keep his commands.
Deuteronomy 7:9

Her Page

If I could just take my daughter back into the history of our own family, I could tell her so many times when the Lord kept His promises to us. Here are just a few of them:

Were I to speak and tell of them,
they would be too many to declare.
Psalm 40:5

God's Page

Father, I praise You today for Your faithfulness in our family's life. And I ask that You would inspire and equip *us* to remain true to *You* as well. I pray all these things and more today . . .

The word of the Lord *is right and true;*
he is faithful in all he does.

Psalm 33:4

Prayer and Other Powers

Ezra was a scribe who took a leading role in helping the Jewish people resettle in their homeland after generations of exile in Babylon. This scene from Ezra 8 gives us a curbside view of this triumphant processional. First you see him making sure that the people do everything right with this fresh start God has given them. Ezra wants them to see for certain that they haven't gotten this far on their own. So they stop before setting foot in the city . . . to fast . . . and pray . . . for them . . . for their children:

There, by the Ahava Canal, I proclaimed a fast, so that we might humble ourselves before our God and ask him for a safe journey for us and our children, with all our possessions. I was ashamed to ask the king for soldiers and horsemen to protect us from enemies on the road, because we had told the king, "The gracious hand of our God is on everyone who looks to him, but his great anger is against all who forsake him."
Ezra 8:21–22

Notice this interesting takeaway, though. The term used for "soldiers" in this passage is the Hebrew word *chayil.* That same Hebrew root word is also translated in other Old Testament verses as our English word "virtue." Amazing, isn't it? Like prayer, *virtue* is a word of power, courage, and battle.

WIDER ANGLE

Read Ezra 8:15–36. Watch for verses:
17 (every great task must begin with worship)
28 (the value of being set apart for God's service)
31 (their need and recognition of God's protection)
34 (no one had stolen; virtue had been upheld)

My Page

I know that the call of godly virtue is a call to battle. I know it won't just naturally be won if I stand on the sidelines and watch the battle from afar. I know that this call is an appeal for me to . . .

Be dressed ready for service and keep your lamp burning.
Luke 12:35

Her Page

My daughter probably experiences the pressure of temptation in her life and world more acutely than I do in mine. In order for me to equip her to stand strong as a godly girl, I need to . . .

Be on your guard; stand firm in the faith.

1 Corinthians 16:13

God's Page

Father God, my daughter and I are committed to being women of virtue. But we won't get anywhere without Your help. Today I thank You, Lord, that You have already proved Yourself faithful . . .

Who can find a virtuous woman?
for her price is far above rubies.
Proverbs 31:10 (KJV)

Alien Residents

If our daughters are to stand firm for God in the face of temptation and opposition, we must teach them the arduous balance of living *in* the world without becoming *of* the world. It isn't easy, is it? But the Bible teaches us that our experience on earth is extremely temporary, that our true citizenship is really in another place. And if we're not yet comfortable with this fact ourselves, if we're still a little too tied down to the good things of this earth, we'll have a hard time teaching our daughters how true this is.

Since you call on a Father who judges each man's work impartially, live your lives as strangers here in reverent fear. For you know that it was not with perishable things such as silver or gold that you were redeemed from the empty way of life handed down to you from your forefathers, but with the precious blood of Christ, a lamb without blemish or defect.

1 Peter 1:17–19

This world has a great hold on many people. Most of us would be lying, in fact, to say that we're not very attached at times to our stuff, our fun, and our habits. If we could only realize how much better it will be in heaven, how rich the reward of God's eternal presence, we'd all be able to let go a lot more.

WIDER ANGLE

Read Daniel 3:1–18. Watch for verses:
7 (the timeless motto: "everybody's doing it")
13 (the angry reaction of others to principled faith)
15 (the way faith can strike unbelievers as nonsense)
18 (the ability to believe without visible reward)

My Page

I've experienced enough of this world that I should easily be able to see through its shallow promises. So I won't dwell today on what I have or don't have. I'll recount instead the great things God has done for me:

If anyone loves the world, the love of the Father is not in him.
1 John 2:15

Her Page

If my daughter had been in the shoes of Shadrach, Meshach, or Abednego, would she have followed the crowd? Or stood by her convictions? What would have helped her take a hard stand when it would have been easier to conform?

I have chosen you out of the world.

That is why the world hates you.

John 15:19

God's Page

Lord, I confess to being too worldly minded. I admit that forever is not frequently in my heart. But I long for it to be. I long to be immune to temporary things and longing for Your face. I pray . . .

He has made everything beautiful in its time.

He has also set eternity in the hearts of men.

Ecclesiastes 3:11

A Moral Standard

We talk and wring our hands a lot about our culture's inability to live by an absolute standard of right and wrong. My, it really is surprising how far we've fallen—and how hauntingly close even the *church* has come to resembling the world in its relativism. But are we practicing this truth we so ardently preach? Is there wiggle room for worldliness in our personal opinions? When things come up, when easy way outs are available, when nobody will get hurt, do we still model one-way obedience to our families?

In the beginning you laid the foundations of the earth, and the heavens are the work of your hands. They will perish but you remain; they will all wear out like a garment. Like clothing you will change them and they will be discarded. But you remain the same and your years will never end. The children of your servants will live in your presence; their descendants will be established before you.
Psalm 102:25–28

In order to raise daughters who don't conform to the culture, we as mothers must also be unwilling to conform. We must consistently live by the unwavering standards of God's Word. We must not let our commitment to Him fluctuate, but must stay permanently guided by His truth.

WIDER ANGLE

Read Daniel 6:1–16. Watch for verses:
3 (devotion to one standard made him exceptional)
4 (they couldn't even *make* up a charge against him)
10 (the option of disobeying was a dead issue for him)
16 (he was always known for the God he served)

My Page

When I try to think through a moral issue, what honestly carries more weight? My feelings? My past experiences? My sympathies for the person involved? Or my trust in what God has said?

All your words are true;
all your righteous laws are eternal.
Psalm 119:160

Her Page

I want to talk with my daughter about some situations in my teen years when I conformed to peer pressure and paid the price—when I listened to my friends' advice instead of doing what I knew was right. Here's one I remember:

Watch your life and doctrine closely. Persevere in them, because if you do, you will save both yourself and your hearers.
1 Timothy 4:16

God's Page

Father, Your Word is true and altogether right. There is only one way of looking at things, and that is *Your* way. Help me to make sound judgments, Lord—judgments based on Your Word alone . . .

For I will give you words and wisdom that none of your adversaries will be able to resist or contradict.
Luke 21:15

How Do I Look?

God certainly never intended for us to ignore our appearance. And I'm all for doing the little things that keep us looking our best. But can a healthy desire to remain attractive go over the edge into a need to be noticed? You know it can. I'd be surprised if you don't know some women who have never realized that they are fearfully and wonderfully made, regardless of the readout on the scale or a bad hair day. Many of us actually sense this struggle, but God's Word reveals our victorious solution:

Your beauty should not come from outward adornment, such as braided hair and the wearing of gold jewelry and fine clothes. Instead, it should be that of your inner self, the unfading beauty of a gentle and quiet spirit, which is of great worth in God's sight. For this is the way the holy women of the past who put their hope in God used to make themselves beautiful. ***1 Peter 3:3–5***

So when it comes to beauty, are we more focused on shedding the five pounds we gained over the holidays or having a regular, daily quiet time with the Lord? Are we more focused on making our nail appointment or our weekly Bible study? Is our need for appearing "together" tearing us apart inside?

WIDER ANGLE

Read Esther 2:5–23. Watch for verses:
7 (would this orphan girl use her beauty to define herself?)
12 (what does a day spa have that she didn't have?)
15 (ahh!—simplicity to go along with her stylishness)
20 (a willingness to stay under proper authority)

My Page

How much inner turmoil do I cause myself over my appearance? Am I dealing graciously with the fact that I'm not as young as I used to be? Is this a big deal to me? Really and truly . . .

Charm is deceptive and beauty is fleeting;
but a woman who fears the L*ORD is to be praised.*
Proverbs 31:30

Her Page

I hope my daughter knows—way deep down inside—that God has made her special and unique. How could I help make this a reality in her eyes?

I praise you because I am fearfully and wonderfully made; your works are wonderful, I know that full well.

Psalm 139:14

God's Page

Lord, this lovely girl You've given to me is more precious than I can imagine. I pray, Father, that she would always see herself as beautifully as I do . . . and as *You* do. I pray for her today that . . .

Man looks at the outward appearance,

but the LORD looks at the heart.

1 Samuel 16:7

That's My Girl!

I remember coming face-to-face with the fact that I was pushing my daughter into gymnastics (five years old at the time) for all the wrong reasons. Sure, I wanted her to excel with the hope that it would boost her esteem in future years. But at the time, all it was doing was causing her to cry on the way to class and tell me how she missed playing with her friends. Did a five-year-old really need that kind of pressure? No. But do some of us want our kids to succeed . . . to boost our *own* esteem?

With this in mind, we constantly pray for you, that our God may count you worthy of his calling, and that by his power he may fulfill every good purpose of yours and every act prompted by your faith. We pray this so that the name of our Lord Jesus may be glorified in you, and you in him, according to the grace of our God and the Lord Jesus Christ.
2 Thessalonians 1:11–12

God has put His designer stamp on our daughters—a personalized plan made in *His* image, not our own. So in our prayer time for our girls—for all of our children—we should be asking God to reveal to us whatever we need to know to lead them toward their destiny. They are *His* girls. Make *Him* proud!

WIDER ANGLE

Read 2 Samuel 12:13–23. Watch for verses:
13 (we sometimes use our kids to right our wrongs)
17 (crossing the line between love and manipulation)
22 (our hearts change when we pray for our children)
23 (coming to grips with God's bigger plan)

My Page

In my relationship with the Lord, do I still feel the need to perform for His approval, to work my way back into His good graces after I've disappointed Him? How do I usually do that?

You do not delight in sacrifice, or I would bring it; you do not take pleasure in burnt offerings.
Psalm 51:16

Her Page

Have I been unfairly pushing my child to excel or perform for my approval or the approval of others? I need to confess this to her. If there's one area where I've perhaps been tangling up my own needs with hers, this is it:

I will very gladly spend for you everything I have and expend myself as well.
2 Corinthians 12:15

God's Page

Oh Lord, I pray for healing from any unmet approval needs in my past that I'm trying to meet through my children. And I pray that You will help me wish for her only the purposes You have created *her* for . . .

He who began a good work in you will carry it on to completion.
Philippians 1:6

Getting Serious about Sex

No surprise here: our culture is obsessed with sex. There's no shielding our daughters' eyes and ears from everything, no matter how hard we work to keep their environment and influences pure. As a result of the blatant temptations and expectations they face, far too many girls are straying from God's standards and choosing to have sex outside of marriage. We could almost feel helpless, forced to give up trying, but God's Word and our fierce love for them demands we fight this with everything we have.

Flee from sexual immorality. All other sins a man commits are outside his body, but he who sins sexually sins against his own body. Do you not know that your body is a temple of the Holy Spirit who is in you, whom you have received from God? You are not your own; you were bought at a price. Therefore honor God with your body.
1 Corinthians 6:18–20

Mothers, we must be purposeful in teaching our daughters that their virginity pledges are made to God Himself. And these promises cover not only sexual intercourse but other impure acts, as well. How far is too far? Anything they wouldn't feel comfortable doing with Jesus present. And be assured, He is!

WIDER ANGLE

Read 1 Corinthians 10:1–13. Watch for verses:
4–5 (being a Christian doesn't exempt us from sin)
6 (the Bible helps us clearly see the results of rebelling)
9 (sexual impurity is done right in God's face)
13 (there's always a way out—the sooner, the better)

My Page

Even if I didn't have a daughter, I hope I'd still be this concerned about the sexual impurity that's all around us. The times when I think it affects me the most (or at least when I notice it the most) are when . . .

. . . men who had understanding of the times,
to know what Israel ought to do.
1 Chronicles 12:32 (KJV)

Her Page

How can I encourage my daughter to develop and pursue purity in the midst of a perverse culture? How can I help her avoid finding herself in sexually tempting situations, to build strong and specific boundaries around herself?

Daughters of Jerusalem, I charge you:
do not arouse or awaken love until it so desires.
Song of Songs 8:4

God's Page

Father, I pray for my daughter's sexual protection. I pray that she would not so much be saying no to sin and harm, but rather that she would be saying yes to Your will and Your way. So I pray today . . .

Then I will be blameless, innocent of great transgression.
Psalm 19:13

What Are Friends For?

It delights me to know that from research, teenagers who feel strongly connected to their parents are far less likely to engage in sexual activity. Clearly, we mothers possess great power in influencing our daughters to abstain from sex until marriage. But I am also grateful for another barrier God has provided our girls: the tight bond of healthy, godly friendships that give them safety, accountability, and encouragement. Whatever we can do to help her stay connected to a good bunch of girlfriends, we need to do it!

Two are better than one, because they have a good return for their work. If one falls down, his friend can help him up. But pity the man who falls and has no one to help him up! Also, if two lie down together, they will keep warm. But how can they keep warm alone? Though one may be overpowered, two can defend themselves. A cord of three strands is not quickly broken.
Ecclesiastes 4:9–12

We can look around at the friends God has given *us*, and we know how well they help us stay grounded and on track. For our daughters who are out there every day with their friends, either being helped or harmed by them, a good friend is a priceless possession.

WIDER ANGLE

Read Ruth 1:1–18. Watch for verses:
8 (so many things can happen to break up friendships)
10 (this one girl was not willing to see it end)
11 (friends aren't concerned with what's in it for them)
16 (it's worth the fight to stay close to good company)

My Page

Are my daughter's friends committed to sexual purity? How can I encourage my daughter to remain pure, and teach her to have the boldness to encourage her friends to do likewise?

He who walks with the wise grows wise,

but a companion of fools suffers harm.

Proverbs 13:20

Her Page

What would I tell my daughter if one of her friends *wasn't* being a good influence on her? What would I suggest or insist that she do about it?

I have written you in my letter not to associate with sexually immoral people.

1 Corinthians 5:9

God's Page

Lord, please wrap my girl in a cluster of good friends. And help her see these precious girls as a gift from Your hand, as a tangible expression of Your love for her. You know how she needs them . . .

Dear friends, let us love one another,
for love comes from God.
1 John 4:7

Gotcha Covered?

One day while shopping, I heard a woman ask a sales clerk to help her choose an outfit for her 10-year-old daughter to wear to a birthday party. When the clerk motioned her toward a sheer blouse, the mother said, "But this is see-through." The sales clerk's response? "Have her wear a sports bra underneath. This is what all the girls her age are wearing." By now I'm practically hyperventilating, so I pipe in, "She's going to a *party*, for heaven's sakes, not a *strip club!*" The sales clerk stormed off, but the mother thanked me for confirming what she already knew.

I also want women to dress modestly, with decency and propriety, not with braided hair or gold or pearls or expensive clothes, but with good deeds, appropriate for women who profess to worship God.
1 Timothy 2:9–10

Many mothers have discounted the clothing battle as not worth fighting, a hill that's not worth dying on. Others fear that their daughters might suffer more from not fitting in than from the signal they'd be sending to the watching world. I say it's time we stop burying our heads in the sand while the boys are all turning theirs!

WIDER ANGLE

Read Ephesians 5:1–16. Watch for verses:
3 (not a hint—not even a hint, mind you)
8 (what would "children of light" go out in?)
13 (only God should see what's on the inside)
15 (where's the wisdom in dressing down?)

My Page

Have I consciously decided not to fight the clothing battle? Or is it just something I try not to think about too much? Or is it something we talk about a lot? Here's how I'd describe its importance to me:

I promised you to one husband, to Christ,

so that I might present you as a pure virgin to him.

2 Corinthians 11:2

Her Page

How would I best summarize the way my daughter feels about the modesty issue? Or how her friends feel about it and express themselves? Is it something I should do more about than I'm already doing?

Blessed is the man who does not condemn himself by what he approves.

Romans 14:22

God's Page

Father, I want the purity You have placed in my daughter's heart to show itself in her outward appearance. I want her—and me, too—to be a living, walking example of Your goodness. So I pray today . . .

Rather, clothe yourselves with the Lord Jesus Christ.

Romans 13:14

In Love with Love?

One morning at my favorite coffee shop, I noticed a line on the chalkboard behind the checkout. It read: "What is the meaning of life?" So I politely asked the college-aged cashier, "Are you planning on posting the answer tomorrow?" She grinned and said, "Well, I guess the answer is different for everyone." Still prodding, I turned the question back on her, asking what her answer would be. "The meaning of life is love," she responded. Hmm. I wonder if that's what the 50% of couples would say who got married for love but ended up getting divorced?

I pray that you, being rooted and established in love, may have power, together with all the saints, to grasp how wide and long and high and deep is the love of Christ, and to know this love that surpasses knowledge—that you may be filled to the measure of all the fullness of God.
Ephesians 3:17–19

Only God's kind of love can rightfully claim to be called the meaning of life. Who wouldn't want to know love that "surpasses knowledge," that fills to overflowing every attempt to measure it? This is the only love we can ultimately depend on. If our girls know His love, our girls will have everything.

WIDER ANGLE

Read Romans 8:28–39. Watch for verses:
28 (God will always be by our side)
31 (we are completely safe in His arms)
35 (the uncertainty of life vs. the certainty of God)
37 (the victory and triumph of living in His love)

My Page

Do I feel that I am worth God's love, even at times when I have behaved in a manner that is unlovely? What are some reasons why this may be difficult for me at times?

How great is the love the Father has lavished on us, that we should be called children of God!

1 John 3:1

Her Page

What are some things I've never told my daughter about the width and length and height and depth of the love of God—things I've seen with my own eyes and known in my own heart?

I am telling you what I have seen in the Father's presence.

John 8:38

God's Page

Perhaps the best way to close my time with You today, Lord, is to tell You what Your love and mercy mean to me. I can hardly put it into words, but I think You'll know what I'm trying to say:

For great is your love, reaching to the heavens.

Psalm 57:10

One Love

It's hard for me to believe this now, but I realize that one day, the Lord will probably lead my daughter to one particular person who will become what my husband has become to me: my best friend, my true companion, the love of my life. In the coming years, her expectations about who this person may be and what her life with him may be like will begin to form. But will she know that marriage is merely the investment of a lifetime, while her relationship with Jesus Christ is a relationship for all eternity?

For the Lord himself will come down from heaven, with a loud command, with the voice of the archangel and with the trumpet call of God, and the dead in Christ will rise first. After that, we who are still alive and are left will be caught up together with them in the clouds to meet the Lord in the air. And so we will be with the Lord forever. Therefore encourage each other with these words.
1 Thessalonians 4:16–18

The longer our daughters spend basking in the unfailing love of Christ, the better equipped they'll be to explore other matters of the heart in the future. As mothers, we would be wise to build a fence of protection around our daughters' hearts until Christ's love has penetrated them through and through.

WIDER ANGLE

Read Colossians 3:1–17. Watch for verses:
1 (the rightful place for our deepest longings)
10 (the desire to live up to our Creator's ideals)
14 (love is so much more than a girl-boy thing)
17 (a bathroom mirror reminder if there ever was one)

My Page

As a young girl, to what degree did I fall for the fairy tale fantasy that a man would be able to make me happy? How has that Prince Charming image become a more realistic one for me?

By smooth talk and flattery they deceive the minds of naive people.
Romans 16:18

Her Page

Have I defined the standards for my daughter's dating? Have we talked about it comprehensively enough that she understands my reasons? The next time I bring it up, I want to be sure to say . . .

The noble man makes noble plans,
and by noble deeds he stands.
Isaiah 32:8

God's Page

Lord, I've lived long enough to know that as wonderful as it is to be loved by another, nothing compares to Your love for me. May nothing compare in my daughter's life to her love for You . . .

My flesh and my heart may fail, but God is the strength of my heart and my portion forever.
Psalm 73:26

Live and Learn

One of the purposes of our daughters' adolescent years is to give them a practice field for developing the basic principles of relationships. Sure, they'll make plenty of mistakes as they work their way through the mysterious maze of girl politics, but every experience will teach them something—honing the skills they'll need to be good wives, mothers, and friends. So we need to place a high value on guiding them through the delicate issues of relating to others. We are their best hope of learning these things safely and gently.

Do not forget my teaching, but keep my commands in your heart, for they will prolong your life many years and bring you prosperity. Let love and faithfulness never leave you; bind them around your neck, write them on the tablet of your heart. Then you will win favor and a good name in the sight of God and man.
Proverbs 3:1–4

Many of us go to great lengths in regard to our children's educational pursuits and enrichment opportunities—and that's all fine and good. But no diploma or trophy will give our girls much satisfaction if they haven't learned how to share, wait their turn, and get along. Building these traits is also a worthy investment.

WIDER ANGLE

Read 1 Timothy 4:6–15. Watch for verses:
8 (the value of maintaining priorities and perspective)
11 (if we have children, then we are called to teach)
12 (our kids can start showing godly character now)
15 (evaluating their progress is good for them *and* us)

My Page

How do I feel when I see my daughter struggling with social situations or having trouble getting along with a certain individual? What's my initial reaction to this? Is it what it should be, or not?

Be completely humble and gentle;

be patient, bearing with one another in love.

Ephesians 4:2

Her Page

Am I overly concerned about my daughter's educational future or her success in extracurricular activities? Does she know that I consider it a quality achievement when she makes strides in her character?

Solid food is for the mature, who by constant use have trained themselves to distinguish good and evil.
Hebrews 5:14

God's Page

Thank You, Father, for making every encounter and opportunity an important one in my daughter's life. I pray to You for real insight so that I can help her learn something new from them every day . . .

For what I received I passed on to you.

1 Corinthians 15:3

Ins and Outs

Think back to your growing-up years, and you'll remember well the damage that was inflicted on girls' lives through the ruthless reign of cliques. Since you and I have grown up now and been blessed with daughters of our own, we're getting to live it all over again, to see it up close and *very* personal. No, the clique monster hasn't changed much. It still feeds off a girl's need to fit in. So one of the best ways to keep the harm to a minimum in your child's life is the same as it's always been: to make sure she realizes where her worth truly comes from.

Make it your ambition to lead a quiet life, to mind your own business and to work with your hands, just as we told you, so that your daily life may win the respect of outsiders and so that you will not be dependent on anybody.
1 Thessalonians 4:11–12

Oh, it can be so hard to be the one who's pushed away by an exclusive pack of girls intent on living out their insecurities. It can also be hard to be the popular girl who's wanting to be kind and loving to those on the outside, but fears what it might cost her. It can be hard to play our parental part in this too. But our girls need us to be there, and to always be theirs.

WIDER ANGLE

Read Nehemiah 6:1–16. Watch for verses:
1–2 (ah, the old squeeze play: three against one)
4 (and it keeps on and keeps on, day after day)
9 (there's real strength in knowing God knows)
16 (godly character will always win out in the end)

My Page

I tend to think of cliques as being a teenage problem, but does it really go away after adolescence? Don't I still feel it and see it happening to me today in grown-up circles? Like the other day when . . .

If you harbor bitter envy and selfish ambition in your hearts, do not boast about it or deny the truth.

James 3:14

Her Page

In what ways is the clique thing different today than it was when I was coming along? Or is it just about the same now as it was then, with only the names changed? Does my daughter realize how timeless this problem is?

Those who are near and those who are far away will mock you.
Ezekiel 22:5

God's Page

Father, I ask for Your patience and forbearance when others play lightly with my daughter's feelings. I know You realize how it feels to see Your child being ridiculed and mistreated. So I pray today . . .

May they be brought to complete unity to let the world know that you sent me and have loved them.

John 17:23

What's Behind Your Back?

Our daughters deal with a lot of things that rarely enter into a grown-up's thoughts anymore. Things like how to spend their allowance money, or what to wear to the homecoming dance, or how to remember that the Louisiana Purchase was completed in 1803. But one challenge that still lingers long into adulthood is our insatiable temptation to gossip, to size people up and serve our opinions for supper . . . where our children can hear us . . . and get the wrong idea that gossiping is bad when you're young, but okay when you're older.

All kinds of animals, birds, reptiles and creatures of the sea are being tamed and have been tamed by man, but no man can tame the tongue. It is a restless evil, full of deadly poison. With the tongue we praise our Lord and Father, and with it we curse men, who have been made in God's likeness. Out of the same mouth come praise and cursing. My brothers, this should not be.

James 3:7–10

Many times I have felt conviction from God over words I have spoken, and the Holy Spirit has prompted me to make it right by contacting the person to whom I passed along forbidden morsels and ask forgiveness. This is a painful exercise, but it makes me think twice the next time I'm tempted to gossip.

WIDER ANGLE

Read Luke 5:17–32. Watch for verses:
17 (here they come, looking for something to dislike)
21 (here they go, looking for a corner to whisper in)
30 (here they are, trying to get others to agree with them)
32 (here Jesus is, knowing what He stands for)

My Page

Only I know the real answer to this: Is gossiping a problem to me? Is it something I've seen God overcoming in my life, or is it a temptation I still consistently give in to? How has gossiping affected me?

Reckless words pierce like a sword,

but the tongue of the wise brings healing.

Proverbs 12:18

Her Page

If my daughter ever witnesses me partaking in gossip, it's my responsibility to own up to my sin, tell her I was wrong, and ask forgiveness. I remember a time when I had to do this . . .

A gossip betrays a confidence,
but a trustworthy man keeps a secret.
Proverbs 11:13

God's Page

Dear Lord, I confess to You that gossiping can still worm its way into my desires at times. The only hope I have is for You to transform my heart and fill me with love for You and for others. Help me . . .

When words are many, sin is not absent,

but he who holds his tongue is wise.

Proverbs 10:19

The Real Thing

The more I speak to Christian youth and college students, the more convinced I become of the need for mothers to train their daughters in the importance of Bible study. I mean, maybe it's because the Bible has become so familiar to us that we lose sight of how transforming and illuminating and powerful it is! But there is so much of it to explore, so much that is unfamiliar territory to our girls. It may be unfamiliar to you, too, but imagine what God would do as you explored it together!

Continue in what you have learned and have become convinced of, because you know those from whom you learned it, and how from infancy you have known the holy Scriptures, which are able to make you wise for salvation through faith in Christ Jesus. All Scripture is God-breathed and is useful for teaching, rebuking, correcting, and training in righteousness, so that the man of God may be thoroughly equipped for every good work.
2 Timothy 3:14–17

In too many places our daughters hear that the Bible is untrue, that God is a figment of their wishful imagination. We cannot give these seeds of doubt a chance to take root in their minds. Don't leave this burden and privilege to their Sunday School teachers. Take your daughter into the Word yourself.

WIDER ANGLE

Read Ephesians 6:10–18. Watch for verses:
12 (the reality of our daily struggle)
13 (our desperate need for protection)
17 (a vivid description of the Bible)
18 (the added value of believing prayer)

My Page

Have I let my love for the Bible slip? Am I affected perhaps more than I realize by the constant bashing and questioning of its authenticity by the experts and educators?

The fear of the LORD is pure, enduring forever.

The ordinances of the LORD are sure and altogether righteous.

Psalm 19:9

Her Page

If I were to ask my daughter how many different ways she's heard the Bible discounted and maligned, would I find that these assertions are making an impact on her? Or that she sees them for what they are?

. . . encouraging you and testifying that
this is the true grace of God. Stand fast in it.
1 Peter 5:12

God's Page

Lord God, I trust You and I trust Your Word. Yet I am praying today that You rekindle my love for it. Show me again, Holy Spirit, how precious and indispensible it is . . .

Your promises have been thoroughly tested,

and your servant loves them.

Psalm 119:140

Just You and Me

Just from the fact that you're working your way through this journal, it's obvious that spending time with God and His Word is valuable to you. I'd imagine you're a lot like me—you've known times when carving out time with God was a real challenge, when it was one of the last things you felt like doing or had time for. But we all know, don't we, that the hard-won discipline of Bible study, prayer, and quiet meditation is one of those anchors in our lives. Something we keep coming back to. Something we need.

Blessed is the man who fears the LORD, who finds great delight in his commands. His children will be mighty in the land; the generation of the upright will be blessed. Wealth and riches are in his house, and his righteousness endures forever. Even in darkness light shines for the upright, for the gracious and compassionate and righteous man.
Psalm 112:1–4

Encouraging our daughters to develop this kind of personal, one-on-one relationship with God is so important. Without scolding but with the promise of blessing, we should help them discover the rewards of time alone with God. Whatever help they need, we should give it. It's that necessary.

WIDER ANGLE

Read Mark 4:1–34. Watch for verses:
1 (see the people hanging on His every word)
10 (see Him getting alone with His disciples)
22 (see Him disclosing things hidden and obscure)
33 (see Him giving them everything they needed to hear)

My Page

I have tried before to survive without spending time in the Bible. Before long, however, my days in the desert leave me thirsty and desperate for His Word. Like the time when . . .

The LORD is good to those whose hope is in him,
to the one who seeks him.

Lamentations 3:25

Her Page

How faithful is my daughter in studying her Bible and in prayer? What can I do to model this to her? How can I encourage her to develop this liberating, life-changing habit?

Be still before the LORD and wait patiently for him.

Psalm 37:7

God's Page

Father, draw me away from my crazy schedule and closer to Your side. Let me never begin or end a day without setting aside time for You alone. Show me how, Lord, I pray . . .

Give me understanding, and I will keep your law and obey it with all my heart.

Psalm 119:34

Shall We Pray?

How's your prayer life? I'll admit this is a loaded question. Those of us who struggle with being faithful and consistent in prayer will always react with a tinge of shame and guilt. *Prayer life? WHAT prayer life?* On the other hand, the more potent the prayer warrior, the more certain she is that prayer isn't something to be measured or graded. There's always more to learn and experience. So I'd say the "how's your prayer life" question isn't really a valid one. There's no such thing as a prayer life. *Every* part of life is a matter of prayer.

Hear, O LORD, and answer me, for I am poor and needy. Guard my life, for I am devoted to you. You are my God; save your servant who trusts in you. Have mercy on me, O Lord, for I call to you all day long. Bring joy to your servant, for to you, O Lord, I lift up my soul.
Psalm 86:1–4

Even as adults we can have a hard time breaking out of the prayer box. We can struggle to see it as anything more than what happens between the "Dear Lord" and the "Amen." But God wants us to *remain* in prayer, not to come in and out of it. He wants us to *live* a prayer life, not to *have* a prayer life.

WIDER ANGLE

Read 2 Kings 19:1–19. Watch for verses:
1 (the humility that characterizes a life of prayer)
10 (the temptation to see God as trivial, powerless)
14 (one of the best pictures of prayer in the Bible)
19 (the point and purpose of all true praying)

My Page

What have been the biggest obstacles to making prayer a bigger part of my life? How have I handled them, how have they affected me, and what should I do the next time they come calling?

Get up and pray so that you will not fall into temptation.
Luke 22:46

Her Page

Do I truly pray for my daughter on a regular and consistent basis? And does she know how often her mother is praying for her? How can I help her be sure of this?

Before they call I will answer;

while they are still speaking I will hear.

Isaiah 65:24

God's Page

Lord, as I continue in prayer today, I'm thankful for this opportunity to reflect on Your nearness, Your accessibility, Your incredible love. Thank You for wanting me close, and for . . .

Pray continually.

1 Thessalonians 5:17

Praise You, Lord

I love the idea of praying Scripture aloud to God in the form of praise—not just reading the words and reflecting on what they say, but actively using them as vehicles of worship. In fact, in order for my family to have access to some of these at bedtime, I have printed out a list of verses that speak of God's attributes (a partial list, of course—there's no end to His awesomeness) and placed it on their nightstands. I want these truths about God's character to live in their hearts—to be so near they can taste them.

Your arm is endued with power; your hand is strong, your right hand exalted. Righteousness and justice are the foundation of your throne; love and faithfulness go before you. Blessed are those who have learned to acclaim you, who walk in the light of your presence, O LORD. They rejoice in your name all day long; they exult in your righteousness. For you are their glory and strength.
Psalm 89:13–17

Oh, how I want each of these traits of God's nature—His righteousness, His justice, His love, His faithfulness—*all of them!*—to be more than a list of words I run through without thinking! I want to dwell on each one, get my arms all the way around them, soak their reality deep within my spirit, and praise Him!

WIDER ANGLE

Read Exodus 15:1–21. Watch for verses:
2 (praising Him for what we've both heard and seen)
11 (the absolute incomparability of God our Father)
17 (God's eternal, unchangeable plans and purposes)
20 (the influence of a woman who worships Him)

My Page

Sometimes I'm so aware of how little I really know about God. His Word is so full, and His ways so far beyond mine. Yet I'm glad that God is too big to be fully understood and figured out, because . . .

How many are your works, O LORD!

Psalm 104:24

Her Page

How could I make the wonder of God a more meaningful reality in my daughter's life? Just to get me thinking, I remember a situation that arose recently where I saw God's hand so clearly . . .

For from him and through him
and to him are all things.
Romans 11:36

God's Page

Lord, I don't know why, but I don't always feel like worshiping. Yet because You are so great, so good, so full of glory, You are more than able to break through my hesitance. Today I praise You for . . .

For you are great and do marvelous deeds;
you alone are God.
Psalm 86:10

True Confessions

Confessing our sins is a valuable part of the believer's day. It has to be handled carefully, though. Sure, we often spend way too *little* time being serious and sorry about our sins. Yet if confession tips out of balance the *other* way, we can focus too heavily on our failings, blinding ourselves to the forgiveness and faithfulness of God. Yes, we make a lot of mistakes in an average day. And we should never grow numb or indifferent to that. But our Savior is more than able to heal and to help. Let's confess that, too.

If we confess our sins, he is faithful and just and will forgive us our sins and purify us from all unrighteousness. If we claim we have not sinned, we make him out to be a liar and his word has no place in our lives. My dear children, I write this to you so that you will not sin. But if anybody does sin, we have one who speaks to the Father in our defense.

1 John 1:9–2:1

We must help our daughters deal with this delicate balance—not glossing over their sins as if they were inconsequential, yet not becoming so spiritually tentative that our girls are unable to live boldly for Christ . . . for fear of doing something wrong. Confession within healthy bounds is a key to Christian living.

WIDER ANGLE

Read Micah 6:1–8. Watch for verses:
2 (God's right to deal squarely with our sins)
3 (our need for remembering His faithfulness)
7 (does God really want more than our hearts?)
8 (God's true desire—genuine love and obedience)

My Page

Where do I fall along this line between confessing too little and confessing all over myself? What makes me lean toward one extreme or the other? What have I noticed this doing to my spiritual health?

For I know my transgressions,

and my sin is always before me.

Psalm 51:3

Her Page

What about my daughter? Is she aware enough of her sins to realize her need for confessing them? But is she confident enough in God to go straight to Him with her failures and experience His forgiveness?

Let us, then, approach the throne of grace with confidence, so that we may receive mercy.

Hebrews 4:16

God's Page

Lord, it's me again, confessing my sins before You. But even as I share them, make me even more aware of Your full knowledge of me and Your total forgiveness. So even while confessing my sins, I will praise You today . . .

But with you there is forgiveness;
therefore you are feared.
Psalm 130:4

Thanks a Lot, Really

One of the greatest benefits of being habitual about thanking God for everything—even thanking Him for answering our prayers in ways other than we'd hoped—is this: it's a strong antidote for discontentment. Discontentment results from focusing on the things we don't have or haven't achieved. But contentment comes from doing the exact opposite: focusing on what we *do* have, what we *are* doing, what we *have* achieved with God's help and strength. The quickest way to contentment is through a grateful heart.

Satisfy us in the morning with your unfailing love, that we may sing for joy and be glad all our days. Make us glad for as many days as you have afflicted us, for as many years as we have seen trouble. May your deeds be shown to your servants, your splendor to their children. May the favor of the Lord our God rest upon us.
Psalm 90:14–17

With the demise of manners in our current culture has also gone the loss of gratitude. Too many kids today never stop to say thanks. They feel entitled to blessing. It is my desire to raise a daughter who not only sees her glass as half-full, but who recognizes (thanks be to God) that her cup runneth over.

WIDER ANGLE

Read Luke 17:11–19. Watch for verses:
13 (we don't mind praying when we need something)
16 (a grateful heart makes anyone look a lot better)
17 (Jesus notices those who fail to thank Him)
19 (gratitude is simply an extension of our faith)

My Page

This journaling process is a great way to begin counting and storing up God's many examples of blessing and favor. I'd imagine I could think of several right off the top of my head . . .

. . . rooted and built up in him, strengthened in the faith as you were taught, and overflowing with thankfulness.

Colossians 2:7

Her Page

Is there an interesting, creative way for me to help my daughter see how blessed she's been? What if I helped her get a lot more specific than the usual list of blessings? What are some things she doesn't typically think of to thank God for?

Give thanks in all circumstances,

for this is God's will for you in Christ Jesus.

1 Thessalonians 5:18

God's Page

Lord God, what a wonder that You transform even our hard times into blessings, helping us look back on them with an awareness that You have turned them for our good. Thank You, Lord, for . . .

My mouth will tell of your righteousness,
of your salvation all day long, though I know not its measure.
Psalm 71:15

Their Turn

She's a big girl now. And I'm glad—I really am—but I have to admit, I miss the days when she was small, when things were so much more simple, when she needed me for just about everything. It was hard (I haven't forgotten that part) but it was a sweet, precious season in life. Now I'm in the mid-stages of letting go, watching her soar and dip and spin and fall, but having to let her become more independent. Even in her relationship with God, I'm having to lead her less to me and more to Him.

God can testify how I long for all of you with the affection of Christ Jesus. And this is my prayer: that your love may abound more and more in knowledge and depth of insight, so that you may be able to discern what is best and may be pure and blameless until the day of Christ, filled with the fruit of righteousness that comes through Jesus Christ—to the glory and praise of God.
Philippians 1:8–11

While it's a wonderful thing for our daughters to count on us as trusted confidants when they are hurting or in need, we should be careful that the comfort we give them is based in no way on our need to be needed. We should be pointing them in the direction of the One who can mend a broken heart.

WIDER ANGLE

Read John 17:6–19. Watch for verses:
8 (it's our job to entrust Christ's truth to our children)
9 (it's also our job to be constantly praying for them)
11 (be free to voice this request: "protect them, Lord")
15 (prepare them to expect a struggle)

My Page

I remember a time when I was in real need, but instead of flying to the phone or bending the ear of my husband, I went first to the Lord. And He really calmed me down. He showed me . . .

Whoever gives heed to instruction prospers,
and blessed is he who trusts in the L*ORD.*
Proverbs 16:20

Her Page

I want my daughter to feel more and more comfortable going directly to God with her needs and concerns—not automatically going to her friends, her youth pastor, or even to me. I can help her by . . .

I am the LORD your God, who teaches you what is best for you, who directs you in the way you should go.

Isaiah 48:17

God's Page

Lord, I don't know if I'm ready for this. But I ask You to begin preparing my heart to more fully release my daughter at the proper time into Your will, Your care, and Your calling. Show me how to do this, Father. Help me to . . .

I always thank my God as I remember you in my prayers.
Philemon 4

Character Infusion

A spirit of humility. Of reverence. Of purity. Of purpose. Of simplicity. Of commitment. Of diligence. Of servanthood. Of consistency. Of assurance. Of availability. Of loyalty. Of sensitivity. Of compassion. Of tenderness. Of maturity. Of holiness. Of reliability. Of openness. Of self-denial. Of confidence. Of integrity. Of repentance. Of trust. Of submission. Of teachability. Of prayerfulness. Of patience. Of peacemaking. Of compassion. Of leadership. Of generosity. Always be asking God to grow character in your children.

For the grace of God that brings salvation has appeared to all men. It teaches us to say "No" to ungodliness and worldly passions, and to live self-controlled, upright and godly lives in this present age, while we wait for the blessed hope—the glorious appearing of our great God and Savior, Jesus Christ. . . . These, then, are the things you should teach.
Titus 2:11–13, 15

What a privilege it truly is to have one of God's girls so close to our hearts, to know her so well, to be able to see straight through her . . . to her deepest need. The character God grows in her while she's under our watch will be the character she serves Him with for the rest of her life.

WIDER ANGLE

Read 2 Peter 1:3–11. Watch for verses:
3 (everything we need is available in God)
4 (He has promised us a way to stay pure)
5–7 (character builds and bears interest on itself)
8 (it keeps us from missing out on God's best)

My Page

When I look back at the list of character traits from the previous page, I see some that God has helped me to grow in recent years. Others of them, well . . . I keep praying about these:

Grow in the grace and knowledge of our Lord and Savior Jesus Christ.

2 Peter 3:18

Her Page

I can read down that same list of attributes and see the ones my daughter is so strong in. But like me, she struggles with some of these more than others. I need to keep praying for God to give her . . .

We pray this in order that you may live a life worthy of the Lord and may please him in every way.

Colossians 1:10

God's Page

What a patient God You are, Father. Even though You embody these character traits in perfect measure, You continue to work with us, raw clay though we are. I praise You for this, Lord, and for . . .

He will sit as a refiner and purifier of silver.
Malachi 3:3

Walking in Darkness

Are you one of those people who manages to stay calm when calamity strikes? Good for you. I'm even going to go out on an honesty limb here myself and say that I'm amazed how much grace God has given me in this area. But for much of my life, I was the first one to fly into freak-out mode at the sight of adversity. This is still my *natural* reaction to any emergency or ordeal. But I am discovering what it's like to sense the peace of God rallying to my defense. He's there for us . . . if we'll walk with Him.

I will praise the LORD, who counsels me; even at night my heart instructs me. I have set the LORD always before me. Because he is at my right hand, I will not be shaken. Therefore my heart is glad and my tongue rejoices; my body also will rest secure. . . . You have made known to me the path of life; you will fill me with joy in your presence, with eternal pleasures at your right hand.

Psalm 16:7–9, 11

Whether it's the loss of a job, the death of loved one, a prodigal child gone astray, a broken marriage, or (in my case) a child who's a few months shy of getting his driver's license, we can cast our cares on the Lord. We can withstand whatever may come our way. We can walk with Him through the darkness.

WIDER ANGLE

Read Romans 5:1–11. Watch for verses:
2 (God has spared us from the worst tragedy of all)
3–4 (we must see our sufferings for what they are)
5 (our hope in God is a hope well placed)
10 (our Lord is truly in the people-saving business)

My Page

How do I usually react to adversity? I'm not just talking about drop-everything emergencies, but how do I typically respond to most difficulties and inconveniences, even those that drag on for days and months. Am I happy with my attitude?

As you know, we consider blessed those who have persevered.
James 5:11

Her Page

My daughter has come across some tough times in her life. How have we weathered these bouts of failure, hardship, loss, or setback? What would she say she's learned from adversity?

Perseverance must finish its work so that you may be mature and complete, not lacking anything.

James 1:4

God's Page

Lord, I'm certainly not praying for trouble. But I know that trouble is a part of life. And so I bring my present difficulties before You today, asking You to do with them all that You have desired . . .

We are not of those who shrink back and are destroyed, but of those who believe and are saved.

Hebrews 10:39

A Life to Give

When my husband and I were in the market for our first home, we met with a real estate agent to determine how much house we could afford. In the process of identifying our monthly expenses, my husband mentioned the amount of tithe we paid to our church. Stunned, she asked if this regular ten percent expense was negotiable. I'm happy to report that we walked out of her office and never looked back. She apparently didn't realize that the blessings of giving are far more precious than a few hundred extra square feet.

"Will a man rob God? Yet you rob me. But you ask, 'How do we rob you?' In tithes and offerings. . . . Bring the whole tithe into the storehouse, that there may be food in my house. Test me in this," says the Lord *Almighty, "and see if I will not throw open the floodgates of heaven and pour out so much blessing that you will not have room enough for it."*
Malachi 3:8, 10

I've told my daughter that she should not even consider marrying a man who compromises in the area of tithing, because this shows his lack of faith in God. If he will dismiss God's commandment about being sacrificially faithful with his money, what would keep him from treating his marriage vows lightly as well?

WIDER ANGLE

Read 2 Corinthians 9:6–15. Watch for verses:
6 (an analogy that's true no matter how you slice it)
7 (a peek inside the blessed heart of an unselfish giver)
11 (one of the main purposes of money: generosity)
13 (our giving is a telling reflection of our faith)

My Page

How faithful have I been in my giving (in general) and my tithing (in particular)? Is this an ongoing struggle for me, or has it become a much more natural part of my obedience? Why?

Whoever loves money never has money enough.

Ecclesiastes 5:10

Her Page

I want my daughter to know that giving ten percent of her allowance or work money to the church each Sunday is as pure an act of worship as the prayers and praise songs. Does she know this? Is she doing this?

Do not work for food that spoils,
but for food that endures to eternal life.
John 6:27

God's Page

Father, I know that every good thing in my life is the direct result of Your lavish generosity. May You help me be quick to share these gifts of Yours and use them all for Your glory, like when I . . .

. . . so that they may take hold of the life that is truly life.

1 Timothy 6:19

Under the Bridge

I know firsthand the toll that shame and guilt over the past can take on your spiritual life. When the skeletons in my closet began to tumble out, I had a hard time believing that God could actually forgive me for some of the things I had done. But somewhere in the midst of my guilt trip, the Holy Spirit rescued me from getting sidetracked on the side roads, and convicted me that Christ had paid for ALL my sins—at a tremendous price! I then realized that if I let the past control me, Satan would get the victory.

Forget the former things; do not dwell on the past. See, I am doing a new thing! Now it springs up; do you not perceive it? I am making a way in the desert and streams in the wasteland. The wild animals honor me, the jackals and the owls, because I provide water in the desert and streams in the wasteland, to give drink to my people, my chosen, the people
I formed for myself that they may proclaim my praise.
Isaiah 43:18–21

Don't allow Satan to hold you in bondage to your past any longer. Instead, by faith in Jesus Christ, accept His freedom from the spiritual consequences of past sins. When your daughter witnesses a mother whose heart is filled with gratitude at the mere thought of the cross, she will see what grace looks like.

WIDER ANGLE

Read Isaiah 43:18–44:5. Watch for verses:
23 (our sacrifice has already been made, and He's enough)
25 (if God chooses to forget our sins, why can't we?)
3 (He offers pure refreshment for our tired souls)
5 (in the Lord, we have been given a new name)

My Page

Perhaps it misses the point for me to list my past sins and dwell on them again. The only benefit I derive from them is this: they are now monuments of God's grace. Let me think about *that* for a while—how He has redeemed my mistakes:

The grace of our Lord was poured out on me abundantly.
1 Timothy 1:14

Her Page

I know I shouldn't burden my daughter with my regretful mistakes just to make myself feel better. I don't want her to have to carry more than she needs to bear. But is there anything I should relate that would be a help to her?

. . . to bestow on them a crown of beauty instead of ashes.

Isaiah 61:3

God's Page

Dear Lord and Savior, I am made new in You. How can I thank You for mercy like this? Even if my sins have been small in the world's eyes, I know You have still saved me from much. So I praise You today . . .

Whoever lives by the truth comes into the light.

John 3:21

Heritage

Long before I came to know Christ, I was blessed with two sets of godly grandparents who were committed to praying for my lost soul. Since then, I have been blessed with children of my own and have seen each one receive Christ as their Savior. Years ago, I also watched my mother return to her own godly heritage of faith. As I look back at four generations of mothers and daughters in my family, I know we have each traveled different journeys. Yet in the end, we share the same bond of faith in Christ. It is our heritage.

I was young and now I am old, yet I have never seen the righteous forsaken or their children begging bread. They are always generous and lend freely; their children will be blessed. Turn from evil and do good; then you will dwell in the land forever. For the LORD loves the just and will not forsake his faithful ones. They will be protected forever.
Psalm 37:25–28

I don't know whether or not you have a similar family story. But you can be assured and encouraged that you are doing your part—embracing the responsibility for passing down a heritage of faith to your children and grandchildren. Let nothing slow you down. You are living your life's calling.

WIDER ANGLE

Read Deuteronomy 28:1–14. Watch for verses:
6 (the blessing of God surrounds the faithful family)
7 (we are protected by the power of His presence)
10 (a godly heritage is a great example to others)
13 (we are assured ultimate victory in the end)

My Page

I can name the ones who have been most influential in leading me to Christ and setting an example of faithfulness before me:

The LORD's love is with those who fear him,
and his righteousness with their children's children.
Psalm 103:17

Her Page

She may get tired of hearing them sometimes, but I need to continue telling my daughter the true-life stories of faith from our family's heritage. I'm thinking of one right now:

You have given me the heritage of those who fear your name.

Psalm 61:5

God's Page

Heavenly Father, You have entrusted us with Your precious children for a short time. May we be faithful in raising our daughters to know that above all, they are Your girls. I pray specifically today for . . .

I have no greater joy than to hear
that my children are walking in the truth.
3 John 4

Complete your Vicki Courtney collection with these companion products for you and your daughter:

Your Girl
Raising a Godly Daughter in an Ungodly World
0-8054-3053-9

More Than Just Talk
A Journal for Girls
0-8054-3057-1

Find these at your favorite bookstore or online at broadmanholman.com

Yada Yada
A Devotional Journal for Moms

These daily devotions will encourage you in the high calling of motherhood and the many tasks and challenges involved in raising teenage daughters. Each devotional experience includes a page for your personal reflection, a page of discussion starter ideas between you and your daughter, plus a page designed simply for worship and prayer. Each day is really a Bible study in itself, with featured verses to ponder and guided tours through other suggested readings.

THE AUTHOR

Vicki Courtney is the founder of Virtuous Reality Ministries and www.virtuousreality.com, an online magazine for middle school girls, high school girls, college women, and adults. She is a national speaker and the author of several books and Bible studies, including Your Girl, The Virtuous Woman, Virtuous Reality and Get A Life! She resides in Austin, Texas, with her husband, Keith, and their three children, Ryan, Paige, and Hayden.

OTHER HELPFUL WEB SITES

vickicourtney.com—to view Vicki Courtney's current speaking schedule or find information about inviting her to speak.

virtuousreality.com—features online magazines for preteen, teen, college, and adult women. Check out this wholesome alternative to the anything-but-wholesome fashion magazines!

virtuousreality.com/events—for information about upcoming Yada Yada and Yada Yada Junior events or to find out how to bring an event to your area.

virtuepledge.com—encourage your daughters to join the virtue movement!